border to border · teen to teen · border to border · teen to teen · border to border

TEENS IN SOUTH KOREA

Teens in South Korea

by Sandy Donovan

Content Adviser: Danielle Ooyoung Pyun, Ph.D.,
Assistant Professor of East Asian
Languages and Literatures,
Ohio State University

Reading Adviser: Katie Van Sluys, Ph.D.,
Department of Teacher Education,
DePaul University

Compass Point Books ✦ Minneapolis, Minnesota

Compass Point Books
3109 West 50th Street, #115
Minneapolis, MN 55410

This book was manufactured with paper containing at least 10 percent post-consumer waste.

Editor: Mari Bolte
Designers: The Design Lab and Jaime Martens
Page Production: Bobbie Nuytten
Photo Researcher: Eric Gohl
Cartographer: XNR Productions, Inc.
Library Consultant: Kathleen Baxter

Art Director: Jaime Martens
Creative Director: Keith Griffin
Editorial Director: Nick Healy
Managing Editor: Catherine Neitge

Library of Congress Cataloging-in-Publication Data
Donovan, Sandra, 1967–
   Teens in South Korea / by Sandy Donovan.
      p. cm. — (Global connections)
   Includes bibliographical references and index.
   ISBN-13: 978-0-7565-3297-0 (lib. bdg.)
   ISBN-10: 0-7565-3297-3 (lib. bdg.)
      1. Teenagers—Korea (South)——Social conditions—21st century—Juvenile literature.
      2. Teenagers—Korea (South)—Social life and customs—21st century—Juvenile
   literature. I. Title. II. Series.
      HQ799.K6D66 2008
      305.235095195–dc22   2007004900

Visit Compass Point Books on the Internet at *www.compasspointbooks.com*
or e-mail your request to *custserv@compasspointbooks.com*

Table of Contents

Angara

Lena

L. Baykal

Sea of Japan

JAPAN

NORTH KOREA

MONGOLIA

C H I N A

Huang

SOUTH KOREA

Yellow
Sea

East
China
Sea

Yangtze

BHUTAN

NEPAL

BANGLADESH

MYANMAR

Salween

VIETNAM

LAOS

PHILIPPINES

THAILAND

Mekong

KAMPUCHEA

South
China
Sea

INDONESIA

*Bay
of
Bengal*

7

TEENS IN SOUTH KOREA ENJOY THEIR COUNTRY'S UNIQUE CULTURE, WHICH COMBINES OLD ASIAN CUSTOMS WITH TECHNOLOGY FROM THE MODERN WORLD. South Korean teens have learned to take the best of what both the past and the present have to offer. They study as long and hard as any teens around the world. They play sports such as soccer and baseball, and practice martial arts. With their families, they visit churches and temples and practice traditional rituals that honor their ancestors. With friends, they chat on cell phones and hang out in cyber cafes.

Teens make up almost one-quarter of the 48 million people who live in South Korea. What is life like in this densely settled country that bridges past and present?

In an attempt to help their children prepare for the CSAT, South Korean parents spend on average between 666,502 won (U.S.$700) and 951,309 won (U.S.$1,000) in private lessons and tutoring per child each month.

CHAPTER ONE

Success in School

IT'S 8 A.M. ON A THURSDAY AND THE CITY OF SEOUL IS ODDLY QUIET. Normally this would be the height of rush hour in South Korea's capital city. Today, however, stores are opening two hours late, airline flights have been delayed or rerouted, and the police have ordered drivers not to honk their horns. What's going on? Is it a national holiday? A religious celebration or a funeral for an important national leader?

No, today is South Korea's annual college-entrance exam day, which is easily the biggest day of the year for high school students and their parents. About 600,000 high school seniors across the country take the College Scholastic Ability Test each year in November. Students prepare for this test almost their entire lives. Many feel their future success rests on their scores. CSAT scores are used to determine what college or university Korean students can enter. And what college they enter will determine their future jobs and even marriages. Only graduates of the top universities are considered for the country's best jobs, and strong networks

The South Korean government has made more than 4,500 free lessons available over the Internet. Almost all South Korean students preparing for the CSAT sign up for this program.

among former students mean that Koreans often prefer to be friends with and even to marry graduates of similar universities.

As the students approach the schools where they will take the test, they are intensely aware of the importance of the day. The rest of the country is preoccupied with the day's test. Businesses open late to clear the streets so students can make it to the test on time. Traffic is controlled by squads of volunteers and special police units. Police and fire emergency vehicles are used to rush late or sick test-takers to their schools. Cars, planes, and even

schools so they can cheer on their test-taking siblings with signs and chants for good luck and victory.

Preparing Early

South Korean children have the goal of acing the CSAT from their early years. More than half of South Korean boys and girls attend kindergarten from age 3 to 5. Elementary school begins at age 6 and more than 99 percent of the country's population attends. Koreans strongly believe in giving everyone equal opportunities, so the government discourages private schools, and most South Korean children attend public

military testing activities are expected to stay quiet on test morning so they don't distract students. Students' families have been focused on this day for years. In the weeks leading up to the test, parents pray at churches or temples for their children's success. Younger brothers and sisters often camp out outside the

Getting Stuck

In Korean slang, getting admitted to a top university is called "getting stuck." So on the morning of the CSAT test, students sometimes smash *yut*—a sticky candy—onto school gates to symbolize getting a high enough score to get "stuck" to one of Korea's top schools.

yut
(yoot)

The number of students per classroom has dropped from about 62 in 1970 to about 36 in 2000.

schools. Courses and textbooks are paid for by the government at public schools. Classes are often crowded—it's common to have 35 to 40 students in one classroom—but they are usually very orderly. Following rules and acting respectfully toward important people such as teachers are important values in Korean culture.

Inside a typical Korean elementary classroom, children sit in neat rows of desks facing the teacher. Kindergarten classes concentrate on five areas: health (gym and dance), society (history), expression, language, and exploration (math and science). Beginning in the lowest grades, South Korean elementary schools focus more on math and science, and Korean students regularly score higher on international math and science exams than do students in most other countries. Korean children also learn to read and write in *Hangul.* More courses, such as music, practical skills, and etiquette and manners, are added later.

Hangul

Hangul, which means the "Korean language," was developed in the 15th century. At that time, Chinese characters were used to write. The Chinese alphabet, however, was complex, and many uneducated Koreans could not read and write. In 1443 the ruler, King Sejong, gathered a group of scholars to ask them to create a new writing style that would be uniquely Korean. The alphabet originally had 28 symbols, but today only 24 (10 vowels and 14 consonants) are used. Hangul is one of the most logical writing systems in the world. It can be learned in a matter of a few days. This has led to Korea having one of the highest literacy rates in the world—more than 98 percent.

Hangul is written left-to-right and top-to-bottom, like European languages.

What to Wear

It's common to see young Korean students in navy blue school uniforms, but uniforms are not required at all schools. Individual schools choose their own uniforms, and parents take their children to a *gyoboksa*, or uniform shop, to get measured and fitted for uniforms. A typical uniform for boys might include black pants, a white button-down shirt, a black jacket, a gray sweater vest (depending on weather), and a red tie.

gyoboksa
(kyo-bok-sah)

Girls may wear a similar uniform with a black or navy blue skirt instead of pants.

South Koreans start three years of middle school at age 12. Some more serious students start to prepare for the college-entrance exam from the middle school years.

Starting to Prepare

Students used to take an entrance exam to get into middle school. In 1969, the government decided it was too stressful for children and eliminated it. Today 12-year-olds are assigned at random to a middle school in their home district. The better-performing students are sent to academic schools,

Although school uniforms are stylish, they are also expensive. Some can cost more than 300,000 won (U.S.$316) each.

Hanbok

Though most school uniforms in South Korea look like European or American uniforms, students at a few schools wear traditional Korean dress, called *hanbok*. Traditional hanbok for boys consists of a wide-sleeved jacket called a *jeogori*, and baggy pants called *baji*. They are gathered at the waist and ankles. Traditional hanbok for girls is a long wraparound skirt called a *chima*, and a short jacket, also called a jeogori. White was traditionally the most common color for clothes. The upper class wore red, yellow, blue, and black, in addition to white. These five colors represent the five elements in Asian cosmology (fire, earth, water, metal, and wood).

hanbok
(HAHN-bok)

jeogori
(che-gori)

baji
(bah-jee)

chima
(chee-ma)

Because of South Korea's diverse weather conditions, hanbok are made from many materials, including hemp, cotton, silk, and satin.

and the ones who either don't excel in academics or simply prefer to pursue a job-training degree are assigned to trade schools. All middle schoolers study 11 subjects, including math, sciences, literature, and language (Korean and, almost always, English). Students study hard because they know that their grades will be marked in their school activity records. These records, along with scores from exams, are used to decide which high school the students will attend.

Three years of high school begin at age 15, and by age 16, students are asked to select a major, or area of concentration. Majors include humanities

Until recently, most middle and high schools separated boys and girls. However, in an attempt to equalize education, many of these schools are now coeducational.

and social sciences, natural sciences, or vocational (job) training. Vocational majors might specialize in electronics, plumbing, or a craft. Some vocational schools are tied to an individual company, and students can usually work at the company after they graduate.

Some Korean teens go to smaller, specialized high schools for music, art, math, or science. In the more general academic high schools, students take courses including biology, chemistry, physics, computer science, algebra, calculus, Korean, English, literature, history, economics, international relations, psychology, and electives such as Chinese, Spanish, and French languages. While most of the focus is on academics, high school students can also take part in school sports including volleyball, basketball, soccer, cross-country, and swimming.

Most students plan to go on to two- or four-year colleges, and the pressure to get accepted into one of the best-ranked universities is intense. Most teenagers become obsessed with studying. In part, they want to receive good grades, but mostly they study to try to boost their CSAT scores. Even students who don't end up attending college take the CSAT. Test scores, not grades, are the most important factor in getting accepted to college.

Pressure to Study

The pressure to succeed on the CSATs is so great that merely attending school

Serious Students

A lot is expected of students in South Korea, and the pressure to succeed can feel intense. But while students are asked to take on a lot of responsibility, they are also treated with great respect. South Korean high school and university students take their duties seriously, and they are concerned with the well-being of their nation. In 1987, university students were accountable for an overhaul of the country's government. At that time, South Korea had been ruled by military leaders for almost two decades, and many young people did not approve of the way this government favored certain groups and treated others poorly. Students staged protests at universities across the country, and succeeded in bringing about the first democratic election in South Korea's history.

A desire for athletic training and for an understanding of the sports industry led to the first university to concentrate on athletic education in 2000.

is not expected to provide the needed results. South Korean teenagers spend up to 15 or even 20 hours a day, six days a week, studying for or thinking about the test. They attend *hagwon*, or cram school, and take private tutoring lessons to boost their knowledge. In fact, it's not unusual for a Korean teenager to sleep for only five hours a night because of all the studying.

On a typical day, a South Korean high school student gets up at 6 A.M. to have an hour or more of cramming before breakfast and school. At school, classes run from about 8 A.M. to 3 P.M. After school, it's rare for a teenager to hang out with friends or go for a bike ride. Instead, most students head straight

hagwon
(hahk-won)

In 2005, a study revealed that students from higher-income homes scored better on the CSAT. Students whose parents had graduate-level education or higher also tended to get higher-than-average scores.

Stress Fest

The first Anti-CSAT Festival was held in 2003 in Seoul and has slowly been gaining fame. Taking place the evening after the CSAT, festival activities include dances, plays, and speeches from students who took the CSAT. Test-takers and high school dropouts banded together and protested against the narrow education system that focuses only on grades and test scores and ignores students' creativity and personal merits.

from class to mandatory study sessions at school. By 5 P.M., they head home for a quick meal before taking off for a cram school. If they don't have time to go home, they grab fast food before lessons. Some teens attend up to three hagwon a day. If a family can afford it, they send their teenagers to a private tutor for science, math, and English-

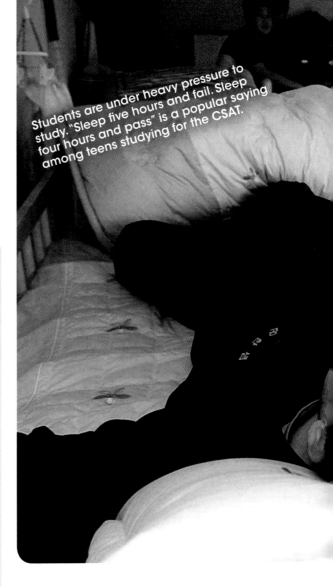

Students are under heavy pressure to study. "Sleep five hours and fail. Sleep four hours and pass" is a popular saying among teens studying for the CSAT.

Vacation School

Although South Korean schools let out for two months each summer, several weeks in December, and usually a week in the fall and spring, teens don't often get much of a break from studying. Many high school students go to special intensive mini-schools during regular school breaks. Sometimes these schools focus on specific topics in which a student needs help. Other times they provide general test-taking practice.

language help. Many teens can be out as late as midnight, studying—leaving no time for family activities or hobbies.

Families encourage their children to study as much as they can. They know that scoring high on the CSAT will

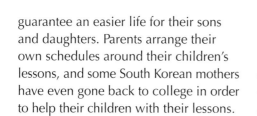

guarantee an easier life for their sons and daughters. Parents arrange their own schedules around their children's lessons, and some South Korean mothers have even gone back to college in order to help their children with their lessons.

Many South Koreans think there is too much focus on studying in their country. Cram schools are a 24.4 trillion won

won
(wohn)

23

(U.S.$26 billion) a year business; one cram school makes more than 154 billion won (U.S.$164 million) a year.

Some Korean parents think there is too much worrying about getting into one of the country's top universities. Others have even moved to other countries to get away from this pressure. One mother who planned to move to Canada explained to a newspaper reporter:

"I'm not satisfied with the education system here. It ruins the family life. Right now my 13-year-old son comes home at midnight because I have to put him in a private institution. I spend about half of my income on education."

The government also tries to limit the focus on private tutoring. The

Teen Scenes

In a small, modern apartment in Seoul, a 15-year-old girl prepares for her day. It's 7 A.M. and she needs to be at school for a study group by 7:45. She hurriedly shoves four thick textbooks into her oversized backpack and heads into the kitchen. Her mother has prepared breakfast for her and reminds her that she needs to eat well to get through her busy day. After school lets out, the girl has two different private lessons, and she won't return home again until after dark.

Meanwhile, in a small town in rural South Korea, another 15-year-old girl embarks on her day. She will also go to school, but first she heads out to feed the family's cows. Then she will begin the 45-minute walk to her country school. She'll return by the same path in the early afternoon, in time to help her father and older brother with afternoon chores around the farm.

Both of these teens lead typical South Korean lives, although the urban lifestyle is far more common in today's South Korea. But despite the difference in their everyday routines, these teens share a love of learning and a knowledge that they must work hard to be successful and make their parents proud.

Studying for the CSAT can be stressful. From 2000 to 2003, more than 1,000 students between the ages of 10 and 19 committed suicide, which was blamed on studying-related stress. Suicide is the fourth leading cause of death in South Korea.

practice of spending a lot of money on private schools goes against the Korean value of equality for all. In fact, from 1980 to the 1990s, most forms of private tutoring were discouraged. But since allowing such tutoring, the government has found it hard to control. In 2005, the government tried to spread equality by broadcasting test study sessions on public television. It also announced that the test would begin to focus mostly on the topics covered during the television study sessions so students attending private lessons would no longer have the biggest advantage.

Celebrating Success

Being a high school student in South Korea is not all work and responsibility. There's also a big party. High school graduation ceremonies are held in June of the third year of high school. South Korean teens' calendars for May and June are usually booked with graduation

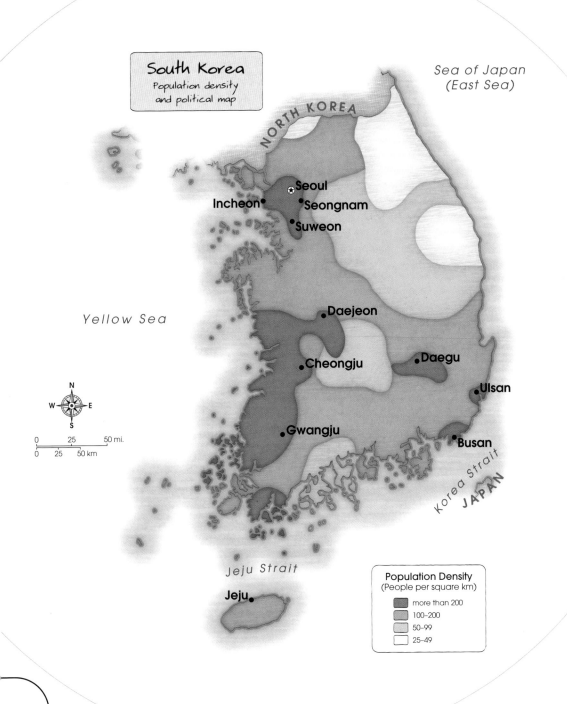

South Korea
Population density
and political map

Sea of Japan
(East Sea)

NORTH KOREA

Seoul
Incheon
Seongnam
Suweon

Yellow Sea

Daejeon

Cheongju

Daegu

Ulsan

Gwangju

Busan

Korea Strait

JAPAN

Jeju Strait

Jeju

N
W   E
S

0   25   50 mi.
0   25   50 km

Population Density
(People per square km)

more than 200
100–200
50–99
25–49

Students who don't get high scores on the CSAT or get into their college of choice may seek additional private lessons and attempt to retake the CSAT at a later time.

parties. Many graduating students have a large party at a restaurant with their family and close friends to help them celebrate. Graduates receive gifts from parents, grandparents, aunts, uncles, and others.

Everybody knows the graduates have worked hard and this is their night to enjoy their success.

Life After the CSAT

Around 25 percent of high school graduates will attend one of the 350 public and private post-secondary schools in South Korea. Other students will attend college in foreign countries. The number of Korean students on college campuses in the United States alone has doubled in the last ten years to 37,000.

Regardless of what their futures hold, South Koreans continue to flock to the cities. Eleven million people live in Seoul alone, and about 80 percent of rural-to-urban migrants choose Seoul as their home.

More than 4 million of the 6 million teens in South Korea have their own mobile phones.

2 Day-to-day Happenings

AT 5 P.M. THE STREETS OF SEOUL BUSTLE WITH PEOPLE. Teenagers carry backpacks or messenger bags crammed with books. Shoppers are heading home too, with food and other purchases in white plastic bags. Over their heads, brightly colored neon signs advertise electronics, cars, furniture, and more. Exhaust from buses floats through the air, while traffic and the ongoing honking of car horns provide background noise to the busy city.

Navigating the crowded sidewalks is a daily routine for most Korean teens, who often head from school to home and then out again to two or three more lessons a day. With more than 80 percent of South Koreans living in urban areas—and about one-quarter of the country's population residing in Seoul alone—South Korea's cities are crowded. But Korean teens have their own ways of tuning out the crowds around them. Walking down the street, they often talk to friends on cell phones or listen to music on their mp3 players.

In Seoul and four other major cities—Busan (also called Pusan), Daegu, Incheon (also called Inchon), and Gwangju—teens might hop on a subway train to get where they're going fast, and to avoid the overly congested sidewalks and busy streets.

Inside the Home

The walls of a South Korean teen's bedroom are covered with posters of his or her favorite bands. A desk is stacked high with textbooks and papers for school. Since the average Korean family has only one or two children, most teens have their own bedrooms.

Around 47 percent of South Koreans live in apartments.

This is where they spend time studying, listening to music, or just relaxing whenever their busy study schedule allows it.

Home for most Koreans in the city is a small apartment in a modern apartment building. The scarcity of available land makes housing very expensive, and therefore apartments tend to be small. A typical apartment has two or three bedrooms, a small kitchen, a combined dining and living room, and one or two bathrooms. These units, built mostly since the 1970s, are quite different from traditional Korean single-family houses that were built of clay and wood. Those houses were held together by wooden pegs instead of nails. New homes no longer have traditional *giwa*, black-grooved clay tile roofs, but they do have running water and electricity, which are not part of a traditional home. Some traditional features have stuck, however. For instance, many modern homes are heated by a centuries-old floor-heating system called *ondol*. Traditional Korean homes had stone pipes under the floors that carried warm air from a kitchen fireplace throughout the home. Today the same system is used in

giwa
(kee-wah)

ondol
(on-dol)

Chores

One side effect of the emphasis on studying in South Korea is that teens aren't expected to do many chores around the house. A Korean teenager's main responsibility is to do well at school and on the college-entrance exam. Families want teens to spend all available hours preparing for exams. So typical Korean teenagers are responsible for keeping their rooms clean, but they are not usually asked to do many other household chores.

South Korean kitchens are slowly moving from traditional cooking spaces to more modernized, technological spaces that will utilize robotics and Internet technology.

most homes, although the heat is now generated by electricity rather than fire.

South Korean homes today are a mix of modern and traditional.

Electronic equipment like microwaves, computers, televisions, and DVD players are found in almost all homes. Nearly 85 percent of all Koreans age

Country Homes

Fewer than one-fifth of South Koreans today live in small towns or villages. Those who do live in small towns and villages tend to have more traditional homes than urban South Koreans. Housing styles vary from the colder northern regions to Korea's more mild south. But most include one large, rectangular living space with a kitchen at one end and a sleeping room at either side. In the south most houses are L-shaped, but in the north they tend to be U-shaped, with a courtyard in the center. Upper-income families might have several smaller houses inside a wall with a lotus pond. Traditionally, one of the buildings was for women and children, one was for the men of the family and their guests, and another was for servants.

14 and over use the Internet. In fact, Korea is a world leader in high-speed Internet connections, with more than 70 percent of its population having a high-speed Internet connection at home. On the traditional side, modern homes have some features from the past. Koreans enjoy simple, sparse furnishing styles that include mats for sitting and low tables for eating. Sitting on floor mats is a Korean tradition, and it allows people to take advantage of the heated floors.

From a young age, Koreans learn from their parents how to receive guests in their home. Traditionally, Koreans greet each other with a bow, and today many Korean teens will bow to their older relatives or their parents' friends when greeting them. After a greeting, a teen might show the guests where to remove and place their shoes, which are almost never worn inside a Korean home. Then the guests will be shown to the most comfortable mats in the house—traditionally families reserve what they consider to be the warmest spot on the floor for guests. The oldest guest will be offered a drink first, then the next oldest, and finally the youngest.

When it's time for a meal, a teenager may be asked to carry a low, portable table out of the kitchen into the living area. The family and guests sit on mats around the table for the meal, in the traditional Korean style. But more and more Korean homes now have a permanent dining table with chairs.

Though South Korean cities have adopted modern architecture, traditional designs are still popular indoors.

At the table

A teenager might grab a quick meal after school in the family kitchen before heading out to a cram school or private lessons. But many families, especially those with young children, sit down for dinner together each evening. Whether they eat at a traditional, low Korean table or a higher table with chairs, it's likely that a family will watch a favorite television program or the evening news together while eating.

A Korean dinner table is crowded with up to a dozen small serving dishes. These are usually small, white, ceramic bowls filled with soups, vegetables, relishes, and sauces. Even a simple weekday family dinner includes one or two main dishes and at least three side dishes. A celebration meal might have up to a dozen small bowls arranged at the table's center. Even fancy Korean meals are served all at once, rather than eaten in courses. Many Korean families still follow the tradition of serving the eldest person first; the oldest person at the table also begins to eat first. Pairs of chopsticks are set on a small ceramic holder at each place. Korean teens know not to display bad manners like spearing food with their chopsticks or crossing them when setting them in the holder. Each place is also set with a spoon. While chopsticks are used for most foods, Koreans use spoons for eating rice.

Rice is one of the two foods found at nearly every Korean meal. The other is *kimchi*, the country's national dish. Kimchi is a hot and spicy dish of pickled vegetables, and the mild, boiled white rice provides a

kimchi
(kim-chee)

Korean food is known for its spiciness. Common seasonings are red pepper, green onion, soy sauce, bean paste, garlic, ginger, sesame, mustard, vinegar, and wine.

Popular varieties of kimchi include cabbage, cucumber, radish, and eggplant. There are also varieties made from fish and fruit.

cooling balance in a Korean meal. Both rice and kimchi reflect Korea's geography and agriculture. Rice is the country's most important crop. The heat and high humidity in the western and southern parts of Korea are ideal for growing rice, and more than half of the country's farmland is used for this staple. Korean cuisine has revolved around rice

for centuries. Kimchi can be made from many vegetables grown in South Korea. The pickling process was developed as a way of preserving summer's vegetables for eating during the region's long, harsh winters. The process also produces a healthy acid that helps people digest their food. Along with the natural fiber and vitamins from the vegetables, this acid makes kimchi a healthful part of the Korean diet.

Soup is another staple at Korean meals. Koreans eat more than 100 varieties of soup. Some are simple vegetable broths, and some have chicken, fish, shellfish, beef, or vegetables in

them. They are eaten both hot and cold, and are usually served in a medium-sized ceramic bowl on the table. Diners serve themselves, putting soup into their own small bowl, and they eat soup with a deep, rounded spoon. They remember to set their spoons down on the table

The Kimchi Refrigerator

Tucked in between the stove and the refrigerator in many modern South Korean kitchens is a uniquely Korean invention: the kimchi refrigerator. This machine has special compartments for pickling and storing batches of kimchi. It is used by families who want to continue to make kimchi at home but don't have the time and materials to do it in the traditional manner. Traditionally, young Korean women learned their own family's kimchi recipe, and then once they married,

they learned their husband's family recipe from their mother-in-law. The process involved cutting up vegetables, mixing them with spices such as red pepper, salt, garlic, and ginger, and burying them in large earthenware jars underground for weeks. While kimchi is still present at nearly every Korean meal, many families now buy a premade version in a jar at a supermarket. Others use a kimchi refrigerator to simplify the process— since a cool, underground burying spot can be hard to find in a modern city.

while using chopsticks and not to make chewing or slurping noises while eating.

South Korean teens today are likely to eat fast food such as hamburgers and fried chicken for some meals. Downtown Seoul has many fast-food restaurants, such as McDonalds, Pizza Hut, and Kentucky Fried Chicken. But at least once or twice a day, teens eat more traditional Korean meals, including rice, kimchi, soup, and other vegetable or meat dishes. Grilling over an open fire

Fast-food restaurants in South Korea offer the regular burger and fries, but also have burgers made with squid, tofu, bulgogi, and kimchi.

In the 1980s, thousands of restaurants that served dog meat were closed after the government prohibited the sale of "foods deemed unsightly." Today these restaurants have started to open again, after a court decision ruled dog meat an "edible food."

is a favorite way of preparing beef and other meat in Korea. Families often go to restaurants where each table has an individual grill for cooking *galbi*, which are barbecued short ribs, or *bulgogi*, strips of marinated beef. The grilled beef, like many other grilled meat dishes found in South Korea, is wrapped with rice in a lettuce leaf. Koreans eat this specialty with their hands. After a meal, Koreans usually enjoy fresh fruit such as sliced pears, oranges, and apples. They rarely eat sugared desserts such as cake or pie, but they do sometimes eat small candies as a snack before a meal.

galbi
(kahl-bee)

bulgogi
(bool-goh-gee)

More families are choosing to have a single child later in life, because of the rising costs and pressure of raising children to succeed, especially in education.

3

Social Networking

IT'S AFTERNOON IN SEOUL, AND 15-YEAR-OLD KIM HO CHIN IS RUSHING AROUND, STUFFING BOOKS INTO HIS BACKPACK. His English language lesson begins in half an hour, and he wants to be on time to ask his tutor a question beforehand. "Have something to eat," his mother calls. "No, I don't have time to eat today," he answers. But his mother hands him *ssam*, a Korean-style burrito made of lettuce wrapped around beef and rice, with a spicy bean paste sauce. "Eat this on the way," she says. "Kam sah hamnida (*thank you*)!" Chin replies as he flies out the door.

South Korean mothers are their children's biggest supporters. Being a high school student in South Korea is demanding, but families view school success as an important family goal. The entire family helps teenagers work toward that goal. In Korean culture, the good of the group— which in this case is the family—is more important than the good of the individual.

ssam
(ssahm)

Kam sah hamnida
(kam-sah-hahm-nee-dah)

This means that family members will do whatever it takes to help their families.

Traditionally, Korean fathers earned the money needed to support their families. Mothers were responsible for raising the children and taking care

Parents play a huge part in their children's academic success, and mothers especially tend to keep close watch on their children's progress.

of the house. This meant that fathers worked outside the house, while mothers usually worked at home to keep things running smoothly. Today many more South Korean mothers—about 50 percent—work outside the house at a paying job. Still, mothers are mostly responsible for setting their children's schedules. Parents may decide together what after-school lessons their teenagers will take. Mothers usually organize the schedules and make sure that their teenagers are on time from one activity to the next.

Ancient Values, Modern Lives

The importance of family in South Korean culture comes from the ancient tradition of Confucianism. Koreans have followed the thoughts of Confucius for about a thousand years as a way of understanding every person's place in society. Confucianism is a philosophy that explains how people should act toward one another based on their relationships. It stresses duty, loyalty, honor, respect for age, and sincerity.

Under traditional Confucian thought, the father was always considered the head of the household. He was expected to provide food, clothing, and shelter for his family members; in return, the family members were expected to obey him. The oldest son was considered the second most important member of the family, and

Country Lifestyle

Although most teenagers in Korea's cities live with only their parents and siblings, close extended families are still most common in the country's smaller towns and villages. Teens who live on farms and in small towns live a more traditional life than their city peers do. They are more likely to live with their grandparents—their father's parents—and their uncles and aunts in one large home.

women were less important. When sons married, they brought their wives to live in their family home. Many generations were able to live closely together because everyone understood, according to Confucianism, what their place in the family was. Everyone understood that their behavior reflected on the entire family's reputation, and so they were careful to act with honesty, respect, and sincerity. Children also understood that they owed their parents a great debt for raising them.

Today in South Korea, it is much less common for many generations of a family to live together. Teens typically

live with their parents and any brothers and sisters they may have. But the teachings of Confucianism still influence how families work. Children know to respect and obey their parents, grandparents, older siblings, aunts and uncles: anyone who is older than they are deserves their respect. Children still feel that their success

at school reflects on their parents and so they work hard to bring honor to the family. A Korean teen might say that she "owes" it to her parents to study hard.

Although teenagers rarely live with their grandparents, they visit them often and treat them with respect. Grandparents tell teenagers stories of

South Korea has been called the most Confucian society in Asia, where respect is prized above all other things.

White Lies

Koreans value honesty and loyalty, so it might seem unlikely that they would tell many lies. But on some occasions, lying is considered the polite thing to do. The concept of losing one's dignity, or losing face, is particularly strong in Korean culture. They use the word *kibun* to refer to a person's pride, mood, and state of mind. It is so important not to hurt someone's kibun that it's better to tell a small lie than to say something that you think might cause another person to lose dignity.

kibun
(ki-boon)

how different life was when they were young—when large families all lived together, homes did not have electricity or running water, and most South Koreans were not as well-off financially as they are today.

One People, Divided

A foreigner visiting a South Korean classroom might see a room full of students with straight, black hair wearing navy and white uniforms. Almost all Koreans share ethnic backgrounds, language, and culture, and they also share many physical attributes. For thousands of years, these people have lived on the land that connects to the Asian continent. Scientists aren't certain, but they believe the original Koreans migrated to the peninsula in prehistoric times. Since then, very few people of other ethnicities have

Korean teens study hard with the hope that they will be able to use their education to give back to their families.

The Look of Modern Korea

Sharing a similar ethnic background, almost all Koreans have naturally straight, black hair. But more and more hair colors are popping up on the streets of South Korea, as teens and young adults embrace hair-dying. Today it's not uncommon to see Korean teens with bleached blond hair, dyed red hair, or even orange-and-yellow-striped hair.

Hair dyes are only one way teens can change their appearance. A BBC journalist in South Korea says, "By conservative estimates, 50 percent of South Korean women in their 20s have had some form of cosmetic surgery." Teens as young as 14 are having surgery to make their eyes look bigger.

moved to the Korean peninsula from the northeastern part of modern-day China. Today some Chinese live in South Korea. But even though they are the largest minority in the country, they still make up less than 1 percent of the total population.

As much as Korean people share, they are also divided. After World War II, two separate Koreas were formed. The Republic of Korea, also known as South Korea, was supported by the United States. To the north, the Democratic People's Republic of North Korea was supported by the Soviet Union. From 1950 to 1953, the Korean War was fought between the two republics, with support from U.S. troops in the south and Soviet troops in the north. Since the 1953 cease-fire, a strip of land 2½ miles (4 kilometers) wide called the Demilitarized Zone has divided the two nations. People are not allowed to cross the DMZ without government permission. Since the division, there has been little contact between North and South Koreans.

Many friends and families were torn apart during the war. Some South Korean teens have relatives living in North Korea whom they have never met. In 2000, the South Korean president visited North Korea for the first time, and the two leaders allowed 100 South Korean families into North Korea to visit. Since then, other visits between family members have been permitted.

Although reunification between

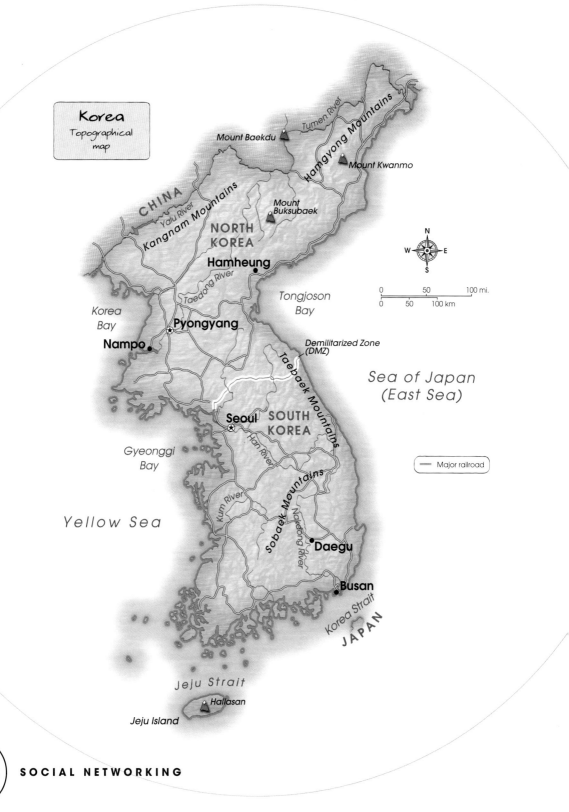

Korea
Topographical
map

CHINA

Mount Baekdu

Tumen River

Hamgyong Mountains

Mount Kwanmo

Yalu River

Kangnam Mountains

Mount
Buksubaek

NORTH
KOREA

Hamheung

Taedong River

N
W   E
S

Korea
Bay

Tongjoson
Bay

Pyongyang

Nampo

Demilitarized Zone
(DMZ)

0   50   100 mi.
0   50   100 km

Sea of Japan
(East Sea)

Taebaek Mountains

Seoul

SOUTH
KOREA

Han River

Gyeonggi
Bay

Major railroad

Yellow Sea

Kum River

Sobaek Mountains

Nakdong River

Daegu

Busan

Korea Strait

JAPAN

Jeju Strait

Hallasan

Jeju Island

North and South Korea are officially still at war. Neither country signed a peace agreement to end the Korean War. The war left both countries in a state of devastation.

the countries has been talked about, the social and economic consequences to both countries have so far prevented any possible joining.

Close Families and Friends

Although most South Koreans may understand the reasons for the North-South split, living as a divided people is hard for Koreans, who place such a high value on family lineage. The Confucian tradition still influences how people live, and South Koreans continue to feel that the family is the most important aspect of life. Ancestors are important, and many families can trace their roots back more than 500 years. Roots and family names are traced through the male line. Koreans typically have three names—the first one is the surname, or last name; the second two are their given names. Women do not take their husband's surname when they marry, and children are given their father's last name only. Confucianism considers males with the same surname part of the same family, no matter how many generations apart they are. Two-fifths of the population have the surnames Kim, Lee, and Park. But not all people with the same last name consider themselves related. Kims from Seoul, near South Korea's northern border, likely belong to a different clan, or extended family, than Kims from the country's southern regions.

Korean teens tend to rely most on their parents and other relatives, but they also have close circles of friends. With such an emphasis on school success, Korean teens don't have time to just hang out with their friends every day, but they do take full advantage of the many electronic communication devices available to them.

After a 12-hour day of studying, many teens connect with their friends

Recently South Korean courts overturned a nearly 700-year-old rule banning marriage between people with the same surname and ancestral line.

Most Popular Names

Popular South Korean first names and their meanings

Boys

Name	Meaning
Chin	The precious one
Chul	Bright
Dae	Greatness
Ha-Neul	Sky
Ho	Tiger, brave
Joo-Chan	Praise the Lord
Jung	Righteousness
Min	Cleverness
Seung	Successor, winning
Sung	Accomplish

Girls

Name	Meaning
Bo-Bae	Treasure, precious
Eun-Joo	Silver pearl
Ha-Neul	Sky
Hea	Grace
Hee	Lady
Jin	Jewel
Moon	Letters
Soo	Outstanding
Sun	Goodness
Young	Distinguished

and family by text messaging, cell phones, or e-mail. Web site chat rooms are another popular way to connect with other teens. Some people say Koreans can seem distant to people they don't know, but once they have been introduced to someone they are extremely friendly. Korean teens are used to being asked personal questions by their friends' parents. It's common for Koreans of all ages to try to figure out where everybody fits in society so they know how to treat them. This carried over from the culture's Confucian roots.

Friendships are important to many Korean teens who may not have siblings in an increasingly single-child society.

More than 800 couples are married every day in South Korea. Many weddings incorporate both traditional and modern ceremonies.

4

Games & Activities

IT'S A WARM MAY DAY, AND THE GRASSY BANKS ALONG A WIDE STREAM IN SOUTH KOREA ARE CROWDED WITH PICNICKING FAMILIES. Small children run around while teens and their parents spread out wheat flour cakes, sliced melon, and other fresh fruit. They also lay out some of the country's most popular picnic food, *gimbap* (rice, carrots, and cucumber wrapped together in seaweed with sausage, fried egg, or fish.) It's Children's Day, and families are celebrating by taking their children to parks, theaters, and zoos. Korean families enjoy spending time together, and celebrating traditional holidays is always fun.

South Koreans celebrate holidays and festivals with food and family. Since they once used a lunar calendar, in which months are set according to the cycles of the moon, many of their holidays are based on lunar months. But they also use the Gregorian 12-month calendar. For instance, while the birthday of Buddha, the founder of

gimbap
(kim–baap)

If the weather allows it, many families celebrate Buddha's birthday and other holidays with a picnic outside.

Holidays

Holiday	Gregorian Calendar	Lunar Calendar
Sollal (New Year)	January 1,2	
Minsok-e-nal (Lunar New Year)	end of January or early February	first day of first month
Samil-jol (Independence movement day)	March 1	
Soka Tanshin-il (Buddha's Birthday)	April or May	eighth day of fourth month
Orini-nal (Childrens Day)	May 5	
Kwangbok-jol (Liberation Day)	August 15	
Kye-chon-jol (National Foundation Day)	October 3	
Song-tan-jol (Christmas)	December 25	

Jumping on a seesaw is a traditional game played during the Lunar New Year.

Buddhism, is usually in April, it is celebrated on the eighth day of the fourth month, which sometimes falls in May. There are also big celebrations for New Year's Day, the Harvest Moon Festival, and other religious holidays.

Two New Years

Imagine following one huge New Year's celebration with another one just a month later. That's what most Koreans do, as they celebrate Sollal, or New Year's Day, on January 1, and then Minsok-e-nal, or Lunar New Year, on the first day of the first lunar month—usually in late January or early February.

The January 1 New Year's festival is the most festive celebration of the year in most South Korean cities, and it often lasts for up to three days. On New Year's Eve, firecrackers and ringing church bells fill the air. Most stores and other businesses close on January 1 and 2, and Koreans spend time with their families. Reflecting the culture's Confucian value of honoring elders, most families have a ritual in which younger members bow to older members to show their respect. Then grandparents and parents give children and teens advice for the coming year and small gifts of money or cakes. On January 2, teens sometimes visit their friends' families or get together to play video games or listen to music.

Dancers perform traditional dances with drums to celebrate the New Year.

The Lunar New Year is often a bigger celebration in rural South Korea than in the cities and towns, where January 1 is more of a holiday. On the Eve of Lunar New Year, families light every room in the home with torches, and then stay up late to protect the new year from evil spirits. The next day, families gather in their best clothes—sometimes traditional Korean clothes, and sometimes more modern outfits. Children and teens bow to their elders to show their respect, and then everybody sits down to a huge feast. This often includes *duggook*, a soup made of rice cakes and dumplings. After the feast, many families play *yut*, a traditional Korean game with wooden blocks and a board.

duggook
(duhg-ook)

yut
(yuht)

Harvest Moon Festival

A long car trip or a journey on the Korea Train Express (KTX) is a typical way to begin Chusok, the Harvest Moon Festival. This early fall holiday is the most popular time for family reunions in South Korea, and parents who have moved away from their parents' families often

Jump rope is traditionally played during the Harvest Moon Festival.

take their children to visit their grandparents on this day. The KTX, which travels up to 185 miles (298 km) per hour, can get them there quickly. In April 2007, the KTX served its 100 millionth customer after slightly more than three years of operation, said the Korea Railroad Corp., which operates the KTX.

The Harvest Moon Festival falls on the 15th day of the eighth lunar month (usually in September or October), and it celebrates the harvest and honors the moon goddess. Koreans have celebrated Harvest Moon Festival for more than 1,200 years. Today families often visit the graves of their ancestors and then gather for a large meal. Traditional Harvest Moon dishes include *songpyon*, which are half-moon-

songpyon
sung p-yohn

shaped rice cakes stuffed with sweet fillings. During the meal, the families offer some of the food to their ancestors' spirits.

Religious Holidays

Korean teens grow up learning about several very different religions that are widely followed in their country—shamanism, Buddhism, Confucianism, and Christianity. Since Koreans have always been open to various faiths and belief systems, it's not uncommon for families to base their own beliefs on several of them and to celebrate holidays of various religions.

From shamanism, the country's oldest belief system, Koreans have borrowed the practices of worshipping nature gods and ancestral spirits. Some teens today even visit fortune-tellers,

Fortune-tellers are taken seriously by some South Koreans: Businessmen want to know about the stock market, mothers ask which colleges their children should apply to, and politicians wonder whether they should run in the next election. A visit to a fortune-teller is also an entertaining activity to do with foreign visitors.

a shamanistic tradition. In past centuries, fortune-telling was practiced by village elders who gave people advice about the future. Today there are more than 60,000 fortune tellers in South Korea. Many of them run Web sites and "zodiac cafes," where teens can get a beverage and have their fortunes told. Some Koreans perform a ritual known as *gut* when they are feeling ill or unhappy. It uses song,

gut
(*guht*)

dance, and prayer to release negative spirits. Most often, teens ask fortune-tellers about their chances of getting into college or about their love lives.

Soka Tanshin-il, or Buddha's birthday, falls on the eighth day of the fourth lunar month, which is usually in April or May. In the past, it wasn't celebrated as a national holiday. But recently, Buddhists declared that since Song-tan-jol, or Christmas, is a public event, Buddha's birthday should be similarly honored. During the day, schools and stores close and teens may go with their families or friends to visit a

Giant lanterns shaped like characters in Buddhist legends are a big part of the Lotus Lantern Festival that celebrates the birthday of Buddha.

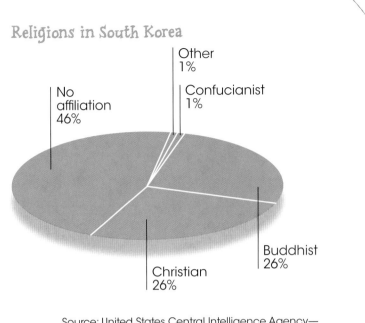

Religions in South Korea

Other
1%

Confucianist
1%

No
affiliation
46%

Buddhist
26%

Christian
26%

Source: United States Central Intelligence Agency—
The World Factbook—South Korea

Buddhism

Buddhists believe that through a life of virtue and wisdom and rejecting worldly possessions, they will find true peace. This ancient religion and philosophy originated in India in 600 B.C., and traveled to Korea around 1,000 years later, in 370 A.D. Over the next 1,000 years, hundreds of Buddhist temples and statues were built throughout Korea. Today about one quarter of South Koreans are Buddhist and still visit and worship at some of the ancient temples and statues.

Christmas is one of the biggest holidays. South Korea is the only East Asian country to celebrate Christmas as a public holiday.

Buddhist temple to make offerings and listen to traditional music. At night parades led by folk musicians wind through the streets toward Buddhist temples. The musicians carry colorful lanterns that are hung up at the temples. Throughout the day and evening, most teens know that their mothers—whether they are Buddhist or not—are praying to Buddha for them to do well on their college entrance exams.

Christmas is the most popular Christian holiday celebrated in South Korea. On Christmas Eve, families sing and listen to Christmas carols together. On Christmas Day, most Christian teens attend church with their families and have a big Christmas dinner.

Christianity

About one-quarter of South Koreans are Christian. In the 1600s, traveling diplomats and Confucian scholars first brought the faith from China to Korea. More Koreans discovered the religion with the arrival of Christian missionaries in the late 1700s and 1800s. The Korean monarchs at that time did not approve of this new religion, and thousands of Christians were persecuted and even killed. Nevertheless, the popularity of Christianity continued to grow, and Korea remained a popular destination for missionaries spreading the word of their religion.

Family Gatherings

Birthdays and weddings are important family celebrations throughout South Korea. For birthdays, gifts and a large meal are common. Teenagers sometimes have two celebrations—one with their families at home or at a restaurant, and another with their friends. Both friends and family members give birthday gifts, and they often closely follow an elaborate gift-wrapping etiquette. Gifts are usually wrapped in red or yellow paper, since these are royal colors, or in yellow or pink, since those colors represent happiness. To avoid bad luck, gift-givers never wrap their gifts in green, white, or black paper, and they never sign cards in red ink, which represents death.

During a traditional wedding ceremony, the bride pours a cup of wine for the groom.

Wedding season in South Korea is spring to autumn. During that time, many popular destinations and hotels that cater to weddings have close to 100 percent occupancy.

The givers also won't see their gifts being opened. It is Korean custom to unwrap gifts in private.

Extended families almost always get together for weddings, which often blend traditional and modern customs. In cities, families frequently rent a wedding hall or hotel ballroom. The bride and groom may wear a white wedding gown and tuxedo for a formal ceremony before entertaining guests at a lavish banquet with music. In smaller towns and villages, more traditional ceremonies remain common, in which the groom travels by horse to the bride's house for a ceremony in traditional clothes. A traditional gift is a pair of mandarin ducks called *wonang*. The birds are often given in pairs, representing the fact that these ducks mate for life. The gift also represents the gift of a long and successful marriage.

wonang
(won-ahng)

Internet cafés are popular places for people to send e-mails, chat, search the job market, and trade stocks online. Some cafés report more than 3,000 customers a day.

5 Into the Working World

YOU WON'T FIND MANY SOUTH KOREAN TEENS RUSHING TO AN AFTER-SCHOOL JOB. While they're in high school, they're expected to concentrate on studying and passing their exams. But that doesn't mean South Korean teens aren't thinking about work. They feel pressure to do well in high school so they can go to a university, and then get a good job.

South Korea's economy is strong—there are plenty of jobs to go around, and the unemployment rate is very low, about 4 percent. But in a society where status is so important, South Korean teens understand that getting into a good college is necessary to get a shot at the country's top jobs—the ones in which they will earn the most and enjoy the most respect from peers. For most of the 20th century, business in South Korea has been dominated by a small group of very large, powerful firms, called chaebol.

chaebol
(che-bohl)

These organizations produce most of the goods in South Korea and enjoy the benefits of the healthy economy. Employees at these firms earn decent salaries and are respected by everyone. But these companies prefer hiring people who graduated from one of South Korea's top universities. Students who graduate from less elite schools or who don't go to universities will likely find jobs, but they will have to work in less pleasant conditions and earn lower wages.

Modernizing Workplaces

No matter how much pressure South Korean teens and young adults today feel about getting good jobs, they know that for the most part they have it easier than their parents did. In the decades

Powerful Chaebol

Since the 1960s, several dozen chaebol have been the business leaders in South Korea. These large, family-owned companies were able to become so successful by receiving government aid. The four most powerful chaebol, often called the "Big Four," are:

Samsung Group: makers of Samsung electronics

LG Group: also electronic producers

Hyundai: cars, ships, and construction manufacturers

SK Corporation: chemical, financial divisions, and telecommunications

following World War II (1939–1945) and the Korean War (1950–1953), South Koreans struggled hard to rebuild their country. Many people worked 12-hour days, six days a week, in factories producing fabrics and processed foods. Their hard work paid off, and from the 1960s through the 1990s South Korea flourished. Its gross domestic product jumped from 9,344 won (U.S.$10) per person, per year to 9,344,960.37 won (U.S.$9,945). It was during this time that the chaebol were at their most powerful. Workers felt great allegiance to their employers, who in turn promised lifetime job security. But in the 1990s, when economies throughout Asia weakened, South Korea went into a deep depression. Businesses failed, banks closed, and thousands of workers lost their jobs.

Since then, South Korea has rebuilt

Hyundai Motor Co. is the number-one car manufacturer in South Korea. One of its three plants within South Korea employs 34,000 workers and produces 5,600 cars a day.

In 1997, South Korea signed an agreement with a global organization asking to receive a nearly 54 billion won ($U.S. 57 million) loan after the economy crashed in the early 1990s. The crash caused mass layoffs throughout the country as businesses fired workers who had devoted their lives to their jobs.

I'M Fired.
정리해고 강요하는
IMF 반대한다
민주노총

itself into one of the world's wealthiest nations, one in which the chaebol have less influence. Workers no longer feel that they need to work at the same company for their entire lives. In the past, it was nearly impossible for smaller-name companies to attract high-ranking businesspeople. Today, however, this has changed. "You can now get good people from the top schools and conglomerates," says the president of Locus Corp., a thriving company started by a local businessman. Also, some newer companies are beginning to hire people based on their skills and work habits rather than which university they attended.

Perhaps the biggest change is that working 12-hour days for six days a week is no longer the norm. Korean leaders were concerned that so much work was damaging citizens' health and lifestyles and in 2004 the government called for shorter workweeks. Large companies introduced a five-day workweek. Smaller companies began giving employees two Saturdays a month off. The government passed a law stating that all companies must have five-day workweeks by 2011.

Employees earn the same amount for a five-day week that they did for their old six-day schedule, but many are having trouble adjusting to their new free time. Some companies have even started teaching former "workaholics" how to relax by taking weekend trips and joining groups such as garden clubs. Many workers, however, are finding their new free time stressful. Some parents are having trouble figuring out how to plan or pay for new activities, while others are feeling crowded at home. One stay-at-home mom said about her husband's shorter workweek: "Home is supposed to be women's space and I don't like it when he spends more time in my space. It's like an invasion." Still, many teens are finding that their working parents now have more free time, and seeing their parents relax away

Some companies have days when employees are allowed to wear offbeat attire. Others are offering short, blind-date style vacations for single employees and specially planned weekend activities.

Some South Korean teens may need to work to pay for school tuitions, books, cell phones, games, or clothes.

from work more often makes them less stressed about their own work futures.

What are the Jobs?

Although they may worry about what kind of job they will get, South Korean teens have many choices when it comes to employment. Almost half of all South Koreans work in the services sector. This includes any business or government body that provides services instead of goods. Tourism, banking, retail, insurance, and postal jobs are all service jobs. Teens who don't go to college may get a job selling goods in a grocery store or in one of the country's many indoor malls. Graduates of technical colleges may get a job repairing office equipment in a service-related company. University graduates may be recruited to run

Labor force by occupation

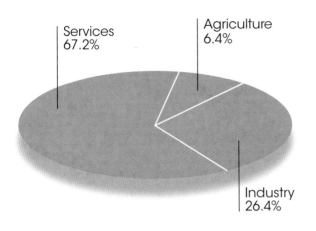

Services
67.2%

Agriculture
6.4%

Industry
26.4%

Source: United States Central Intelligence Agency—The World Factbook—South Korea

service companies, movie theaters, or stores.

Many other Korean teens pursue careers in manufacturing. After the services sector, manufacturing employs the highest number of South Koreans—just over one-quarter of all workers. The country has some of the most modern factories in the world, and they produce and export ships; cars (Hyundai and Kia are based in Korea); steel; electronics such as computers, televisions, and audio devices; and other goods such as clothes and running shoes.

Reaching the SKY

The group that consists of South Korea's three top universities—Seoul National University, Korea University, and Yonsei University—is nicknamed SKY. Only the highest scorers on the college-entrance exams are admitted to these schools, but once admitted, students believe they have it made. There is a strong network among former students. Successful business leaders mentor and help those who graduate from the same university they attended. SKY graduates often land the most prestigious and best-paying jobs in the country.

Rice accounts for 45 percent of a farmer's income. This may drop as more rice is imported from other countries.

Military Service

South Korea has five branches of national military—the army, navy, air force, marine corps, and national maritime police—and teens are eligible to volunteer for military service at age 18. Between ages 20 to 30, all Korean men must complete mandatory military service of 24 to 28 months, depending on the branch.

Teens who grow up in South Korea's rural regions may become farmers. For most of the country's history, farming was the most common occupation. Children who grew up on farms almost always worked on them and eventually took them over. Today rural teens are just as likely to move to a city to go to a university, or to find work in a factory or store. Only about one-tenth of all South Koreans work on farms. With so many mountains, less than one-quarter of the country's land is suitable for farming. Half of all farmland is used to grow rice, the national crop. Other farms grow corn, soybeans, or other fruits and vegetables, or produce chickens, ducks, or pigs.

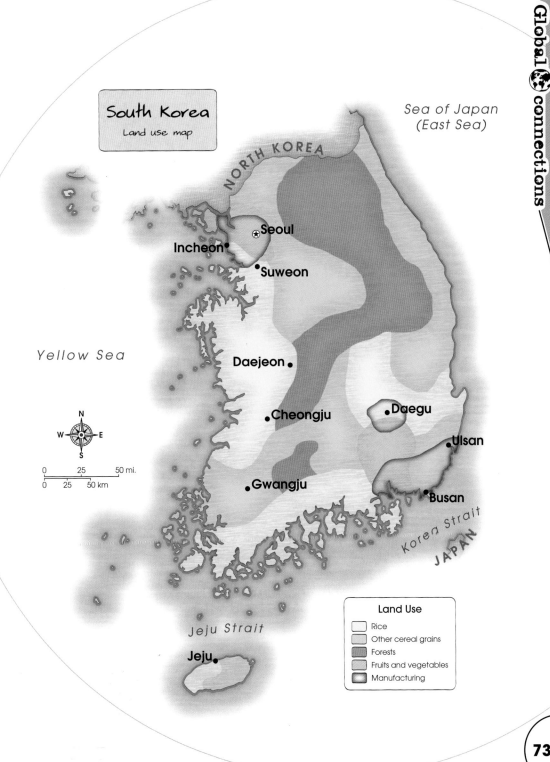

South Korea
Land use map

Sea of Japan
(East Sea)

NORTH KOREA

Seoul
Incheon
Suweon

Yellow Sea

Daejeon

Cheongju

Daegu

Ulsan

Gwangju

Busan

Korea Strait

JAPAN

N
W E
S

0   25   50 mi.
0   25   50 km

Jeju Strait

Jeju

Land Use

Rice
Other cereal grains
Forests
Fruits and vegetables
Manufacturing

Video games are a popular pastime in South Korea. The government spends about 95 billion won (U.S.$100 million) a year to promote, research, and develop the video game market.

6

More Time for Fun

THE BASE OF A MOUNTAIN NEAR THE CITY OF JEONJU, IN WESTERN SOUTH KOREA, IS CROWDED WITH ACTIVITY ON A SUNDAY MORNING. Along the grassy slopes, groups of hikers gather. A dozen 15-year-olds, members of a hiking club, form a circle to plan their day's route. Their goal is to reach the peak's summit, where a triangular-shaped rock juts out toward the sky. Just below the jutting rock, a long, narrow, steel suspension bridge stretches to a nearby hill. Over the course of this spring day, more than 500 hikers will cross it. There will be other hiking clubs, families, and groups of co-workers—young, old, and every age in between. The youngest and the oldest will stay near the wide trails on the mountain's lower half. The more experienced and physically fit will venture to the top.

With more than 70 percent of its land covered by mountains, hiking is South Korea's most popular outdoor activity. But South Koreans also like to take advantage of their country's lush landscape for other outdoor activities. In the summer, groups of teens

South Korea has more than 1,700 hiking trails available year-round. Most are free, or offer inexpensive passes.

may head to one of the many rivers or streams to fish. Skiing has been a popular winter activity for several decades, but today many South Korean teens prefer snowboarding. Most Korean ski resorts didn't allow snowboarding until about 2000, and since then it has caught on fast with teens across the country.

Organized Sports

Walk near an open field in any South Korean town on a Sunday afternoon, and you will probably see teens playing soccer. The sport was brought to Korea in the 1880s by the British, and in 1983 South Korea became the first Asian country to have a professional soccer team. Soccer exploded in popularity after South Korea co-hosted the World Cup soccer tournament in 2002. Although South Korea was eliminated by Germany in the semifinals, the event produced millions of young soccer fans in South Korea. Today most Korean teens follow the world soccer scene.

Korean teens play other international sports, too. Baseball is another favorite with teens. Korean teens apply themselves to sports with the same intensity they use for studying. When they play in competitions, they work hard and excel. In 2000, for example, the South Korean Little League team beat the U.S. team to win the gold medal at the AAA World Junior Baseball championship in Canada. Basketball, volleyball, and table tennis are also popular.

The most hardcore soccer fans are called the "Red Devils." More than 2 million fans turned out to watch South Korea's semifinal match with Germany at the 2002 World Cup.

Korea also has a rich history of traditional sports and competition. The best known traditional sport is taekwondo, a self-defense martial art. Contestants use rapid-fire hand and foot movements in this 2,000-year-old sport. Many teens manage to squeeze in hours of sparring—practice fighting—each week to master this demanding sport. It became recognized as an Olympic sport

Taekwondo requires the use of the entire body. Tae means "to kick," kwon means "punching" or "destroying with the hand or fist," and do means "way" or "method."

Olympic Hosts

Seoul hosted the Summer Olympics in 1988, instilling pride in teens and adults across South Korea. More than 8,400 athletes from 159 countries attended the events. South Korean athletes won 12 gold medals and 10 silver medals, but the Korean people's real sense of pride came from showing off their land and culture to the world. The country built 12 brand-new showcase arenas and gymnasiums, and remodeled dozens more, to provide a world-class setting for the competitions.

in 2000. South Korean athletes won three gold medals that year, and two more at the next Olympics in 2004.

The Sound of K-pop

Sports competitions aren't the only events that inspire devotion from South Korean teens. On any given weekend, the Gymnasium Arena in Seoul's Olympic Park—or any one of dozens of other arenas across the country—is crowded with thousands of teens and young adults screaming at the sight of their favorite pop stars. South Korea's booming pop music scene is known around the world as K-pop. It is not one unique sound, but includes music that draws on Asian, American, and European styles of rap, rock, and techno. Shows are usually high-tech productions with lasers, fireworks, or other special effects. K-pop superstars are cultural sensations throughout Asia and have played to sell-out crowds in Europe and North America.

K-pop is not the only South Korean popular art finding huge success around the world. Since 2000, Korean-made television shows and films have built large audiences across Asia. In fact, the popularity of K-pop music, television dramas, and films has been so extraordinary that journalists have coined a term to describe it—the "Korean Wave." It has been compared to the "British Invasion" of the 1960s, when the Beatles and other British pop culture acts took the rest of the world by storm.

Cyber Game Capital

It's a sunny, bustling afternoon on the streets of the southern city of Busan. But inside a darkened room the only light is the flickering of computer screens, and the only sound is the electronic swish of cyber swords slicing opponents. You're inside a South Korean PC *baang*, or online game center. South Korea is the online

PC baang
(PC bahng)

Musical Role Models

As K-pop becomes more and more popular, South Korean teens have more and more famous role models to look up to.

Rain

Sometimes called the Korean Justin Timberlake, Rain was the first Korean artist to perform in the United States. He has won several Asian music awards and honors. In February 2006, he played two sold-out nights in New York City's Madison Square Garden.

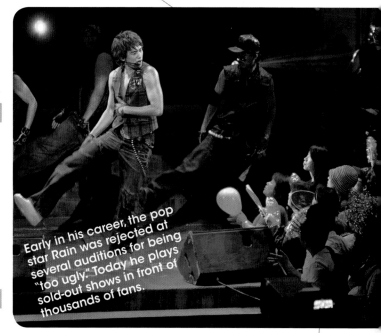

Early in his career, the pop star Rain was rejected at several auditions for being "too ugly." Today he plays sold-out shows in front of thousands of fans.

BoA

This female singer has sold more than 10 million albums. She won the Most Influential Artist award at the MTV Asia Music Awards in 2004. The next year she became the first non-Japanese singer in more than two decades to reach number one on the official Japanese music charts.

Se7en

After four years of intense training under his management agency, he released music in both Japan and Korea. In 2006, Se7en won Favorite Korean Artist at the MTV Asia Awards.

gaming capital of the world, and almost all South Korean teens have at least tried this cyber pastime. Because the country has such readily available high-speed Internet connections—which are needed because of the intense graphics of the games—Korean teens play computer games online instead of using software or video game consoles. Online games can last for days and the hobby is becoming so trendy across South Korea that some adults are concerned that teens are wasting too much time on it. Kim In Kyung landed her dream job as an internationally ranked video game player. Her parents still don't understand what her job is. "They don't know I'm living in the Internet world," she says, "They just know I have a good job." But the teens who play say they love the intense concentration required to play, and that it helps them unwind from the pressure of school and studying. In 2001, Seoul hosted the world's first "Cyber Olympics," where more than 400 players from 37 countries competed in computer gaming. Many popular Asian players receive sponsorships that allow them to practice their video game skills full time. The best players can make more than 1.42 million won (U.S.$150,000) a year from prizes and sponsorships.

About 18 million South Koreans play video games every year, fueling an 8.2 billion won (U.S.$8.7 million) industry.

Looking Ahead

AT HOME, AT SCHOOL, AND AT PLAY, SOUTH KOREAN TEENS HAVE A RANGE OF OPPORTUNITIES. They embrace both their culture's rich traditions and the accessories of modern technology. They may trace their ancestors back for more than 500 years, yet they routinely use cutting-edge technology, including mp3 players, cell phones, and other personal electronics. It's not uncommon for a South Korean teen to spend part of the day wearing traditional hanbok before changing into a shirt emblazoned with a favorite K-pop star.

Although teens make up almost one-quarter of South Korea's population, their numbers are shrinking as families have fewer and fewer children. Teens know it will soon be up to their small generation to guide the nation.

As their country completes its evolution from a traditional farming society to a world-class leader in manufacturing and technology, today's South Korean teens look forward to a bright future.

At a Glance

Official name: Republic of Korea

Capital: Seoul

People

Population: 48,846,823

Population by age group:
0-14 years: 18.9%
15-64 years: 71.9%
65 years and over: 9.2%

Life expectancy at birth: 77 years

Official language: Korean

Other common language: English

Religion:
No affiliation: 46%
Christian: 26%
Buddhist: 26%
Confucianist: 1%
Other: 1%

Legal ages
Alcohol consumption: 21
Driver's License: 18
Employment: 18
Leave School: 15
Marriage: 18
Military service: 18 for voluntary, 20–30
for compulsory of 24–28 months
Voting: 19

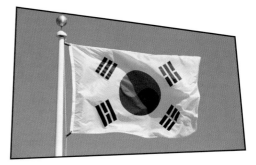

Government

Type of government: Republic

Chief of state: President, elected

Head of government: Prime Minister, appointed by president, with approval from National Assembly

Lawmaking body: Kukhoe, Unicameral National Assembly, elected

Administrative divisions: Nine provinces

Independence: August 15, 1945 (from Japan)

National symbol: Flag is white with a red and blue yin-yang symbol in the center; there is a different black trigram from the ancient *I Ching* (*Book of Changes*) in each corner of the white field

Geography

Total Area: 38,023 sq mi (98,480 sq km)

Climate: temperate; more rain in summer months

Highest point: Halla-san, 6,435 feet (1,950 m)

Lowest point: Sea of Japan (East Sea), sea level

Major rivers: Gum, Han, Nakdong, Seomjin, Youngsan

Major landforms: Mountain ranges Charyeong, Jiri, Sobaek, Taebaek

Economy

Currency: South Korean won

Population below poverty line: 4%

Major natural resource: coal

Major agricultural products: rice, root crops, barley, vegetables, fruit, cattle, pigs, chickens, milk, eggs, fish

Major exports: semiconductors, wireless telecommunications equipment, motor vehicles, computers, steel, ships, petrochemicals

Major imports: machinery, electronics and electronic equipment, oil, steel, transport equipment, organic chemicals, plastics

Historical Timeline

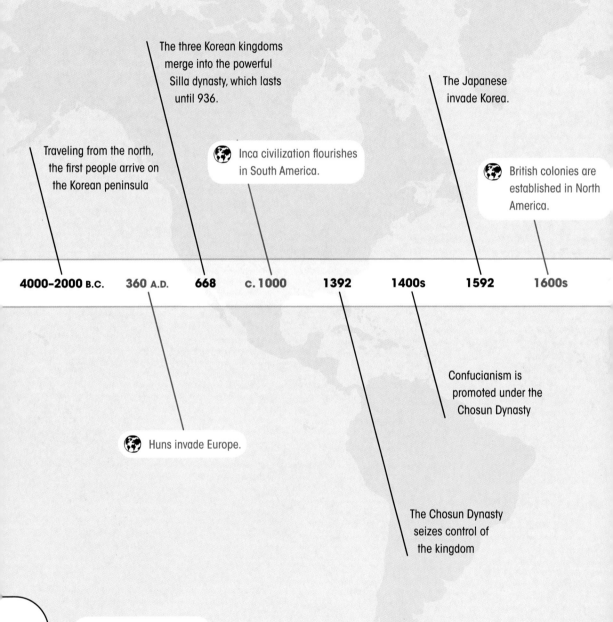

The three Korean kingdoms merge into the powerful Silla dynasty, which lasts until 936.

The Japanese invade Korea.

Traveling from the north, the first people arrive on the Korean peninsula

🌎 Inca civilization flourishes in South America.

🌎 British colonies are established in North America.

4000–2000 B.C.	360 A.D.	668	c. 1000	1392	1400s	1592	1600s

🌎 Huns invade Europe.

Confucianism is promoted under the Chosun Dynasty

The Chosun Dynasty seizes control of the kingdom

🌎 Historical World Event

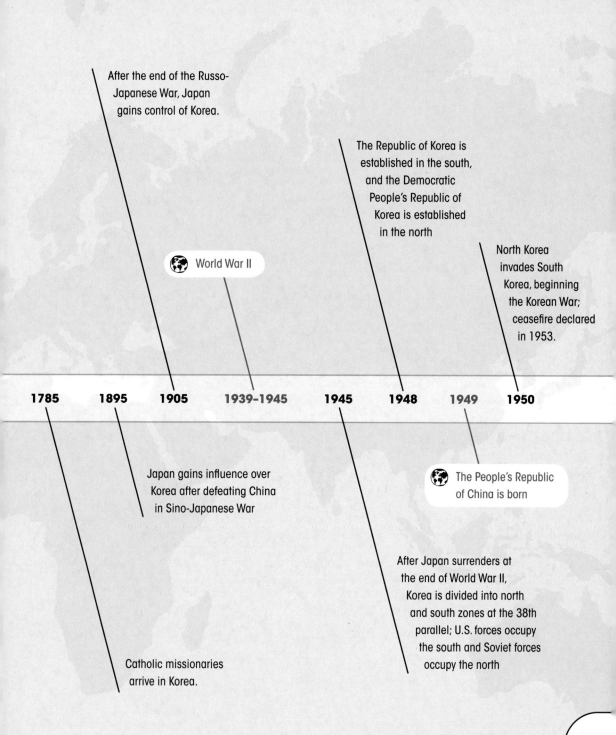

After the end of the Russo-Japanese War, Japan gains control of Korea.

The Republic of Korea is established in the south, and the Democratic People's Republic of Korea is established in the north

🌐 World War II

North Korea invades South Korea, beginning the Korean War; ceasefire declared in 1953.

| 1785 | 1895 | 1905 | 1939–1945 | 1945 | 1948 | 1949 | 1950 |

Japan gains influence over Korea after defeating China in Sino-Japanese War

🌐 The People's Republic of China is born

Catholic missionaries arrive in Korea.

After Japan surrenders at the end of World War II, Korea is divided into north and south zones at the 38th parallel; U.S. forces occupy the south and Soviet forces occupy the north

Historical Timeline

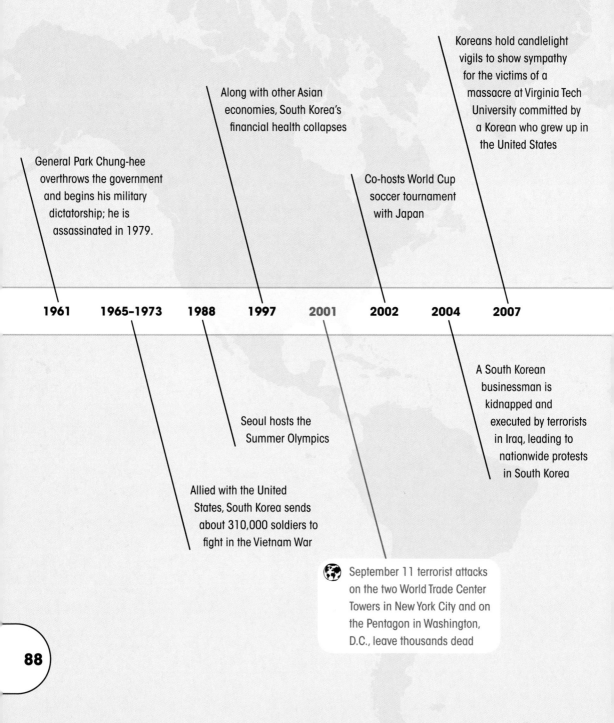

Koreans hold candlelight vigils to show sympathy for the victims of a massacre at Virginia Tech University committed by a Korean who grew up in the United States

Along with other Asian economies, South Korea's financial health collapses

General Park Chung-hee overthrows the government and begins his military dictatorship; he is assassinated in 1979.

Co-hosts World Cup soccer tournament with Japan

1961　　**1965–1973**　　**1988**　　**1997**　　**2001**　　**2002**　　**2004**　　**2007**

A South Korean businessman is kidnapped and executed by terrorists in Iraq, leading to nationwide protests in South Korea

Seoul hosts the Summer Olympics

Allied with the United States, South Korea sends about 310,000 soldiers to fight in the Vietnam War

September 11 terrorist attacks on the two World Trade Center Towers in New York City and on the Pentagon in Washington, D.C., leave thousands dead

 Glossary

democratic | government in which the people elect their leaders

dictator | ruler who takes complete control of a country, often unjustly

diplomat | person who represents a community or government in its foreign affairs

economy | country's systems of trade and finance

ethnic | having to do with a group of people sharing the same national origins, language, or culture

evolution | gradual change into a different form

mandatory | required by someone in authority or a government

manufacturing | the process of producing goods, often in factories

network | system or people or things that cross or connect

Additional Resources

IN THE LIBRARY

Fiction and nonfiction titles to further enhance your introduction to teens in South Korea, past and present.

Choi, Sook Nyul. *Year of Impossible Goodbyes*. Boston: Houghton Mifflin, 1991.

Kim, Richard E. *Lost Names: Scenes From a Korean Boyhood*. Berkeley: University of California Press, 1998.

Park, Linda Sue. *When My Name Was Keoko*. New York: Clarion Books, 2002.

Lee, Cecilia Hae-Jin. *Eating Korean: From Barbecue to Kimchi, Recipes from My Home*. Hoboken, N.J.: Wiley, 2005.

Salter, Christopher L. *South Korea*. New York: Chelsea House Press, 2005.

Sang-Hon, Choe, and Christopher Torchia. *Looking for a Mr. Kim in Seoul: A Guide to Korean Expression*. Infiniti Press, 2006.

ON THE WEB
For more information on this topic, use FactHound.
1. Go to www.facthound.com
2. Type in this book ID: 0756532973
3. Click on the Fetch It button.

Source Notes

Page 24, column 2, line 2: Jeremy Garlick. "Flying Toward New Dreams." *The Korea Herald.* 24 May 2002.

Page 39, photo caption, line 5: "Korea Dog Meat Row Hots Up." BBC News. 27 Jan. 2007. 25 April 2007. http://news.bbc.co.uk/1/hi/world/asia-pacific/1785106.stm

Page 47, photo caption, line 4: Scanlon, Charles. "The Price of Beauty in South Korea." BBC News. 3 Feb. 2005. 25 April 2007. http://news.bbc.co.uk/2/hi/programmes/from_our_own_correspondant/4229995.stm

Page 57, column 1, line 6: "KTX Bullet Train Passengers Top 100 Million After 3 Years of Operation." The Republic of Korea Official Website. 25 April 2007. http://korea.net

Page 68, column 2, line 2: Brian Bremner and Moon Ihlwan. "Korea's Digital Quest." Businessweek Online. 25 Sept. 2000. 24 April 2007. www.businessweek.com/2000/00-39/b3700015.htm

Page 69, column 1, line 32: Lina Yoon. "More Play, Less Toil Creates Stress for Some Korean Families." *The Wall Street Journal.* Accessed through Pittsburgh Post-Gazette, 10 Aug. 2006. www.post-gazette.com/pg/06222/712558-82.stm

Page 81, column 1, line 17: Brian Bremner and Moon Ihlwan. "Korea's Digital Quest." Businessweek Online. 25 Sept. 2000. 24 April 2007. www.businessweek.com/2000/00-39/b3700015.htm

Pages 04-05, At A Glance: United States. Central Intelligence Agency. *The World Factbook—Korea, South.* 17 April 2007. 24 April 2007. www.cia.gov/cia/publications/factbook/geos/ks.html

Select Bibliography

Asia Media. "Koreans on Internet for 13 hours a week." *Korea Times*. 9 Aug. 2006. 18 Aug. 2006. www.asiamedia.ucla.edu/article-eastasia.asp?parentid=50609.

Breen, Michael. *The Koreans: Who They Are, What They Want, Where Their Future Lies*. New York: Thomas Dunne Books, 2004.

Card, James. "Life and death exams in South Korea." *Asia Times Online*. 30 Nov. 2005. 1 Sept. 2006. www.atimes.com/atimes/Korea/GK30Dg01.html

Chung-a, Park. "Students hold anti-exam festival." *The Korea Times*. 24 Nov. 2005. 19 Nov. 2006. http://times.hankooki.com/lpage/200511/kt2005112419013968040.htm

CIA World Factbook Online. *South Korea*. 30 Nov. 2005. 3 Sept. 2006. www.cia.gov/cia/publications/factbook/print/ks.html

Dae, Cheong Wa. "About Korea." *Korea's Office of the President*. http://english.president.go.kr/cwd/en/korea/Korea_01.html?m_def=5&ss_def=1

Dudley, William, ed. *Opposing Viewpoints: North and South Korea*. Farmington Hills, Mich.: Greenhaven Press, 2003.

Faiola, Anthony. "When Escape Seems Just a Mouse-Click Away: Stress-Driven Addiction to Online Games Spikes in S. Korea." *The Washington Post*. 27 May 2006. www.washingtonpost.com/wp-dyn/content/article/2006/05/26/AR2006052601960.html

Fulford, Benjamin. "Korea's Weird Wired World." *Forbes*. 21 July 2003, p. 46. www.forbes.com/technology/free_forbes/2003/0721/092.html

Garlick, Jeremy. "Flying Toward New Dreams." *The Two Koreas, Vol. 76, Number 3*. New York: H.W. Wilson, 2004.

Gateway to Korea. "Educational System." Korea.net. 12 Jan. 2007. http://korea.net/korea/kor_loca.asp?code=F0202

Kim, Dayhawk. "Children Suffer From English Fatigue Syndrome." *Global Pulse*. 26 June. 2006. 11 Nov. 2006. www.globalpulse.net/archives/asia/children_suffer_000217.php

Kwintessential Language and Cultural Specialists. "South Korea—Language, Culture, Customs and Etiquette." www.kwintessential.co.uk/resources/global-etiquette/south-korea-country-profile.html

Peloso, Jennifer, ed. *The Reference Shelf: The Two Koreas*. New York: H.W. Wilson, 2004.

"South Korea Timeline." *Time For Kids*. 11 Oct. 2006. www.timeforkids.com/TFK/hh/goplaces/article/0,20343,927456,00.html

Timeline South Korea. 14 Jan. 2007. http://timelines.ws/countries/KOREASOUTH.HTML

Yoon, Lina. "More Play, Less Toil Creates Stress for Some Korean Families." *The Wall Street Journal*. 10 Aug. 2006. Accessed through *Pittsburgh Post-Gazette*, 15 Sept. 2006. www.post-gazette.com/pg/06222/712558-82.stm

Index

About the Author
Sandy Donovan

Sandy Donovan has written several books for young readers about history, economics, government, and other topics. She has also worked as a newspaper reporter, a magazine editor, and a Web site developer. She has a bachelor's degree in journalism and a master's degree in public policy, and lives in Minneapolis, Minnesota, with her husband and two sons.

About the Content Adviser
Danielle Ooyoung Pyun, Ph.D.

Our content adviser for this book, Danielle Ooyoung Pyun, is an assistant professor in the Department of East Asian Languages and Literatures at Ohio State University. She has taught courses on Korean language and Korean culture. She is also interested in developing language materials as well as doing research on the Korean language. Currently she is working on a textbook for adult learners of Korean.